December 1989.

KU-739-183

# Let's Celebrate

Oxford University Press, Walton Street, Oxford OX2 6DP

Oxford  New York  Toronto
Delhi  Bombay  Calcutta  Madras  Karachi
Petaling Jaya  Singapore  Hong Kong  Tokyo
Nairobi  Dar es Salaam  Cape Town
Melbourne  Auckland

and associated companies in
Berlin  Ibadan

*Oxford* is a trade mark of Oxford University Press

© John L. Foster 1989
First published 1989

All rights reserved. No part of this publication may be reproduced,
stored in a retrieval system, or transmitted, in any form or by any
means, electronic, mechanical, photocopying, recording, or otherwise
without the prior permission of Oxford University Press.

This book is sold subject to the condition that it shall not,
by way of trade or otherwise, be lent, re-sold, hired out or
otherwise circulated without the publisher's prior consent in any
form of binding or cover other than that in which it is published
and without a similar condition including this condition being
imposed on the subsequent purchaser.

British Library Cataloguing in Publication Data
Let's celebrate.
I. Foster, John
808.81

ISBN 0 19 276083 1 hardback
ISBN 0 19 276085 8 paperback

Typeset in Meridien by Pentacor Ltd, High Wycombe, Bucks
Printed in Hong Kong

# Let's Celebrate

## Celebrate

### FESTIVAL POEMS

COMPILED BY

## John Foster

OXFORD UNIVERSITY PRESS

OXFORD    NEW YORK    TORONTO

# Contents

## Festival

First of all
Fast of all,
Feast of all –
Festival

*John Kitching*

## Once Upon a Great Holiday

I remember or remember hearing
Stories that began
'Once upon a great holiday
Everyone with legs to run
Raced to the sea, rejoicing.'

It may have been harvest Sunday
Or the first Monday in July
Or rockets rising for young Albert's queen,
Nobody knows. But the postman says
It was only one of those fly-by-days
That never come back again.

My brother counted twenty suns
And a swarm of stars in the east,
A cousin swears the west was full of moons;
My father whistled and my mother sang
And my father carried my sister
Down to the sea in his arms.

So one sleep every year I dream
The end of Ramadhan
Or some high holy day
When fathers whistle and mothers sing
And every child is fair of face
And sticks and stones are loving and giving
And sun and moon embrace.

*Anne Wilkinson*

## First Foot

One . . . . two . . . . three . . . . four . . . .
Midnight knocking at our door.

A tall dark stranger waits outside
Turning away, his face to hide.

A lump of coal in one black hand –
What does it mean? Why does he stand

Holding his other hand out to us all
As we welcome him into the midnight hall?

Goodbye to the old year, good luck in the new,
'Come in, dear friend, peace be with you.'

*Ian Serraillier*

*This refers to one of the New Year rituals traditionally observed on January 1st in Scotland and other parts of the United Kingdom. A dark man will 'bring the new year in' by visiting his friends as the old year ends. The gift of coal is to wish them 'warm home, warm hearts'.*

# My New Year's Resolutions

I will not throw the cat out the window
Or put a frog in my sister's bed
I will not tie my brother's shoelaces together
Nor jump from the roof of Dad's shed
I shall remember my aunt's next birthday
And tidy my room once a week
I'll not moan at Mum's cooking (Ugh! fish fingers again!)
Nor give her any more of my cheek.
I will not pick my nose if I can help it
I shall fold up my clothes, comb my hair,
I will say please and thank you (even when I don't mean it)
And never spit or shout or even swear.
I shall write each day in my diary
Try my hardest to be helpful at school
I shall help old ladies cross roads (even if they don't want to)
And when others are rude I'll stay cool.
I'll go to bed with the owls and be up with the larks
And close every door behind me
I shall squeeze from the bottom of every toothpaste tube
And stay where trouble can't find me.
I shall start again, turn over a new leaf,
leave my bad old ways forever
shall I start them this year, or next year
shall I sometime, or . . . . .?

*Robert Fisher*

*At New Year some people make New Year's Resolutions – a list of things they should or should not do – and then see for how long they can keep to them.*

## *Dragon Dance*

A Chinese dragon's in the street
And dancing on its Chinese feet
With fearsome head and golden scale
And twisting its ferocious tail.
Its bulging eyes are blazing red
While smoke is puffing from its head
And well you nervously might ask
What lies behind that fearful mask.
It twists and twirls across the road
While BANG the cracker strings explode.
Don't yell or run or shout or squeal
Or make a Chinese dragon's meal
For, where its heated breath is fired
They say it likes to be admired.
With slippered joy and prancing shoe
Why, you can join the dragon too.
There's fun with beating gongs and din
When dragons dance the New Year in.

*Max Fatchen*

*The Chinese New Year begins on the first day of the first moon (February or March). The New Year processions are led by a huge dragon, made of bamboo covered in paper or silk, which is a symbol of good luck.*

## Lion Dance

Drum drum gong drum
gong gong cymbal gong
gong she fah chai
cymbal clang drum clash
gong she fah chai
lion saunter lion strut
gong-she gong-she
yellow body bright eye
gong she fah chai
eye wink eye flash
cymbal clang drum clash
lion coy lion cute
she-she she-she
lion lie lion sleep
fah chai fah chai
fah chai fah chai
gong she fah chai
man walk man creep
gong she fah chai
lion wake! lion leap!
gong she fah chai!
lion angry lion cross
gong-gong she-she fah-fah chai-chai
lion leap lion high
chai! chai! chai! chai!
people cower people fly
gong chai! gong chai!
*lion pounce lion prance*!
*gong gong gong gong gong gong gong gong*
*gong she fah chai*!
*gong gong gong gong gong gong gong gong*
**GONG SHE LION DANCE!!**
**GONG SHE LION DANCE!!**

*Trevor Millum*

*The lion dance is performed in Singapore on many occasions, especially at Chinese New Year. It is accompanied by extraordinarily loud clashing percussion, which sets up an exciting rhythm to the movements of a highly stylized lion. Inside the lion are two very acrobatic and hot dancers! 'Gong she fah chai' is 'Happy New Year' in Mandarin. This poem is meant to be performed by two voices or sets of voices.*

# Waitangi Day

A thousand years ago, or maybe more,
    Canoes bring people to this land,
    Land of the long white cloud;
With paddles and sails they tame the ocean,
    Golden-brown people from distant islands,
    The vikings of the sunrise.
Why do they come here, Maori people?
    What do they hope for? What do they seek?
    New homes, new hunting grounds, new lives.
No humans dwelt here till this time,
    But many fish swim in these waters,
    And on the shores are strange birds:
The kiwi and the giant moa roam,
    Running birds that do not fly,
    Laying eggs as big as coconuts . . .
Long after this, two hundred years ago,
    *Pakeha* come, white men with awesome magic,
    In boats as large as seven canoes,
Bringing spears that spit out fire;
    Then Maori people fall and die,
    And the lives of the living change . . .
So comes a time of many troubles,
    A time for bitter memories,
    Lands are taken, wars are fought,
Until a day when white men meet with chiefs,
    At Waitangi on the Bay of Islands;
    The place where a treaty is made.
Now, each summer when the sun is high,
    On this day they call Waitangi Day,
    There is feasting and rejoicing.
What is past cannot be changed,
    But the old ways are remembered:
    Crafts, words, dances, songs . . . *Maoritanga*.

*David Bateson*

*Waitangi Day is New Zealand's national day, celebrated each year on February 6th. It marks the Maori treaty with the European settlers.*

## *Corroboree*

Hot day dies, cook time comes.
Now between the sunset and the sleeptime
Time of play about.
The hunters paint black bodies by firelight with
    designs of meaning
To dance corroboree.
Now didgeridoo compels with haunting drone
    eager feet to stamp,
Click-sticks click in rhythm to swaying bodies
Dancing corroboree.
Like Spirit things in from the great surrounding
    dark
Ghost-gums dimly seen stand at the edge of
    light
Watching corroboree.
Eerie the scene in leaping firelight,
Eerie the sounds in that wild setting
As naked dancers weave stories of the tribe
Into corroboree.

*Kath Walker*

*Corroboree is the festival dance performed by the aborigines of Australia.*
*Music is provided on the didgeridoo – a wind instrument.*

## Corroboree

The clap, clap, clap of the clapsticks beat
By the old, red rocks with their scars
To the stamp, stamp, stamp of the old men's feet
And the wink, wink, wink of the stars.
With the drone, drone, drone of the didgeridoo
And the sound of its ancient tune
In the dance of the snake and the kangaroo
By the light of the walkabout moon.
The chants will rise and drift and fall
While the night with a magic fills
Where the old men dance to the Dreamtime's call
In the heart of the secret hills.

*Max Fatchen*

## Fishing Festival

Into the river
            jump, man!
Jump –
        jump in!
Carry your net
            and fish, man –
gathering
        tail and fin.
He who catches
    most shall be
known for his
    dexterity
and rewarded
    he will be –
Jump!
        Jump in!

*Jean Kenward*

*The Kebbawa people of north-western Nigeria celebrate the start of the fishing season by gathering on the banks of the Sokoto river, carrying calabash dippers and butterfly fishing nets. Then everyone jumps in the river together, so that the fish are startled and leap into the nets and dippers.*

## *February 14th*

I like that boy
in Mrs. Jones's class.
I like his face.

He doesn't know
me, although
when we
were in the playground
I thought he
looked at me.
Once.

I could give him
some secret
sign. I know his
address. He'd
never guess
who sent
a Valentine.

*Ann Bonner*

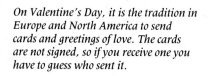

*On Valentine's Day, it is the tradition in
Europe and North America to send
cards and greetings of love. The cards
are not signed, so if you receive one you
have to guess who sent it.*

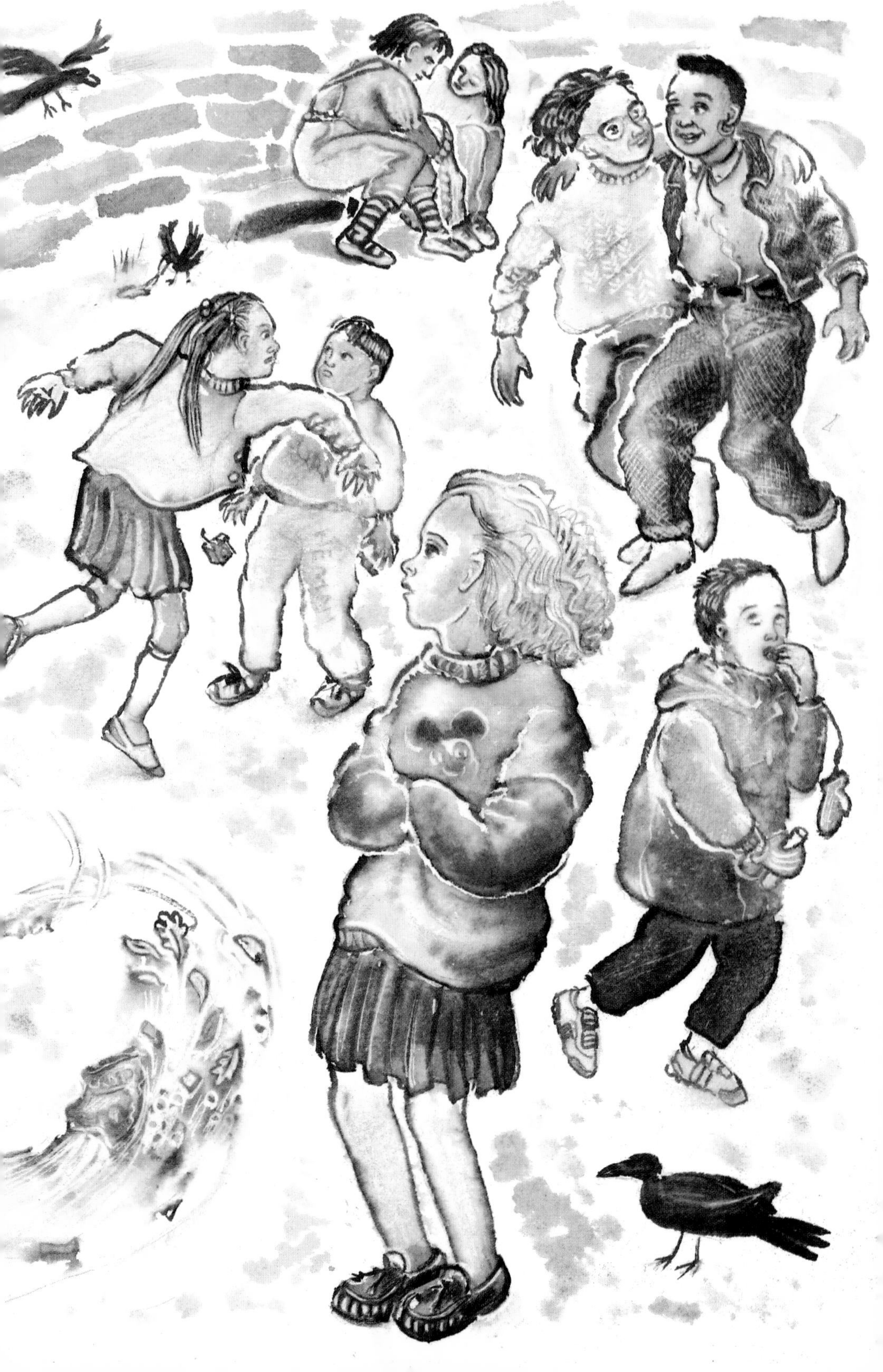

# Shrove Tuesday
## (A Movable Feast)

Beat the batter
in the bowl.
Heat the butter
in the pan.
Toss the pancake
if you can.

In the Shrovetide
pancake races
pancake experts
show their paces.
Pancakes dropped
or held aloft.
Pancakes proud.
Pancakes flopped.

With watering mouths
and hunger hearty
we will have
a pancake party.
Cram as many
as you can –
some with treacle
some with jam.
Pancakes fat.
Pancakes neat.
Piles of pancakes.
Eat. Eat, eat.

*Ann Bonner*

*Shrove Tuesday is the last day before the period which Christians call Lent – the forty days
leading up to Easter when they remember the time Jesus spent fasting in the wilderness.
People used to give up things in Lent, such as eating butter or eggs. So it became the
tradition on Shrove Tuesday to use up all your butter and eggs by making pancakes.*

# *Mardi-Gras*
## *(West Germany)*

Come and join the Carnival
    Carnival
        Carnival
Come and join the Carnival,
all the people say!

Blow your trumpet
  wear your hat
and if you are
  thin or fat
who is there
  to care for that?
The clowns are down
  our way!
Singing, dancing,
feasting, vaulting,
stamping, laughing,
somersaulting . . . .
Come and join the Carnival,
it's Mardi-Gras today!

*Jean Kenward*

*The Tuesday before Lent is also called Mardi-Gras. In Germany it is the day of Carnival – the last chance to have some fun before Lent starts. In Brazil, Carnival is the most important holiday of the year.*

## *Carnival in Rio*

Rumba rumba
    carioca rumba
rumba all day O
    rumba all night
with everywhere a rumba
    carioca rumba
rumba everybody
    everybody rumba
rumba rhythm O
    rhythm of the rumba
rhythm of maraccas O
    red-hot maraccas
    rattling maraccas O
carioca rumba carioca rumba
    frantic moans
    of saxophones
and the laughing bones
    of xylophones
to the rhythm of the rumba
    carioca rhythm
    carioca rumba
rhythm of the rumba
    rum and cocacola
razzle-dazzle razzle-dazzle
    white smiles
    razzledazzle
      high hats
    razzledazzle
sequins feathers pearls
    razzledazzle
birds of paradise
    masks of crystal
    carioca rhythm
    carioca rumba
rumba rumba rumba rumba
rumba all day O
    rumba all night . . .

*James Kirkup*

## *King of the Band*

Between the iron, the steel and the ding-o-lay
I see
the king of the band
Only so high
but already a professional
in motion
A woman standing next to me
jabs me in the ribs
   Look, look nah! De boy really know how to dance
he costume.
The feathers and the sequins take on a life
of their own
You're swaying to the music
they doing something else
They're jamming

Cloaked in turquoise and purple
scarlet and the shades of wonderment
the colours do more than reflect the sun
they splinter the rays snatching at
globules of the melting gold like
voracious fire-eaters
then belch them back with the
same intensity
into the furnace of a
Caribbean afternoon
The process is a never ending one of
separation, absorption and expulsion

Martyr for the day
Your headdress is an ornate structure
of beaten copper studded with gems
A crucifix they must relieve you of
from time to time
Beads of perspiration run like rivulets
down your brows
leaving a pattern of spikes
like the crown of thorns
The paint and the glitter is
now smudged and dirty yet
you're still smiling bravely through
it all

     For

     the videos are on you
     the cameras are on you
     all eyes are on you
and the show must go on
Knowing this
you break into a dance which has them cheering
Impetus at your heel
you grind life into the moisture still
resting from the late morning rain
Steam rises from the soles of your shoes
For today
you are king
you have the world at your feet
For today
you are king
The world lies easy at your feet
For today you are king
The king of the band

*Amryl Johnson*

*In Trinidad, the children's carnival is held on the Sunday before Ash Wednesday. It gives even the smallest child the chance to parade in a costume exotic enough for her or him to be called queen (or king) of the band.*

## Jouvert Morning

The sun. The sun
jumps up on the Savannah, a copper mask, a brazen pan
beating, just jumping, no stopping
its deep bass echoing in the haze that makes the houses
seem to vibrate, belly-out, shift their sides:
and coming with the heat, the thrum and thrust of drums
rising in the dust churned by heavy trucks whose steel
shimmers as they rumble like chariots of thunder
in the ruck and swell, the surge of masqueraders;
a tumbled mass of sailors, kings, red indians and demons,
birds and beasts, gods of cloth and cane and feather
who roll and ripple on the riffs, the bursting waves of brass
breaking on a hoped-for shore where everybody is somebody
and the masks of everyday drop like discarded rotis
to be crushed by the feet of the dancers in the street as
freed and lost inside the tempo they celebrate themselves.

*Dave Calder*

The Trinidad Carnival takes place on the days before Lent. Although there are many
events leading up to it, the carnival proper begins in the night between Dimanche
Gras (Sunday) and Jouvert (I open) Morning and continues till the night of Mardi
Gras (Shrove Tuesday). Although this is held in February, it is the dry season so
near the Equator, and very hot. About 50,000 people dress in costume and dance
through the streets of Trinidad's capital, Port of Spain, to the accompaniment of steel
bands, carried on lorries, that play the year's favourite calypsos.

## St David's Day

The land returns from Winter
Like the Saint from pilgrimage
Bringing with him a bird and a flower
Over mountains like dragons turned to stone.

Today repeats the yearly miracle
Along the valleys of the daffodil
And in the brightening sky above
St David's emblem is the dove.

*Stanley Cook*

*St David is the patron saint of Wales, and March 1st is St David's Day.*

## Saint David's Day

At school they told us
that it was the day
on which Jesus
and a host of angels
came to Wales.

There was sunshine
full of endless song
– and the soul of David
was borne away
to heaven.

I thought,
'He must have been
a good man
for God's Son
to come for him.'

Through the classroom window
we could see late white
linger in patches,
and brave green blades
spearing through
the soggy carpet
of last Autumn's leaves.

And the blades
proudly unfurled
their yellow banners
– their daffodil symbol
of St David
and the heart
of Wales.

*David Watkin Price*

# *Holi*

Under the full spring moon
Lord Krishna
watched young Rahda,
her downy beauty
delicate as pollen in the air,

a slim girl
in the slender light.

Krishna threw powder,
coloured powder
soft and mischievous as love
under the liquid moon;

through shadowed veils
her eyes danced.

New flowers bloomed
next day in Krishna's garden,
frail graceful girls
dancing their stories
to the powdered bees.

*Irene Rawnsley*

*Holi is a Hindu festival. It is a happy, rather mischievous occasion, when children and adults throw coloured powders at each other, recalling how Lord Krishna is said to have thrown powder at young Rahda.*

## The Doll Festival
*(haiku)*

Lighted lanterns
cast a gentle radiance
on pink peach blossoms.

Third day of third month.
Mother brings out five long shelves –
black lacquer, red silk.

On the topmost shelf
we place gilded folding screens
and the two chief dolls.

They are Emperor
and Empress, in formal robes:
gauzes, silks, brocades.

On the lower steps,
court ladies with banquet trays,
samisen players.

High officials, too,
kneeling in solemn stillness:
young noble pages.

Fairy furniture –
dressers, mirrors, lacquer bowls,
bonsai, fans, braziers.

Should the royal pair
wish to go blossom-viewing –
two golden palanquins.

Third day of third month.
Our small house holds a palace –
we are its guardians.

Lighted lanterns
cast a gentle radiance
on pink peach blossoms.

*James Kirkup*

*Long ago, the Japanese used dolls to drive away evil spirits. On March 3rd, Japanese girls*
*celebrate the Doll Festival by creating a royal court, which consists of a set of fifteen dolls on stands*
*draped with red cloth.*

## *Mothering Sunday*

In the times before Bank Holidays
Farmer's boys and servant girls
Left the farm or big house early,
Going home for the day
On Mothering Sunday
Though home was miles away,
With flowers for their mother's present
Gathered as they went.

It's different these days:
All you have to do is stop
At the flower shop
With the pocket money you've saved
And the daffodils there
Came by train or even by plane;
But the present still means the same
For the language of flowers doesn't change.

*Stanley Cook*

*In England, Mothering Sunday is celebrated on the third Sunday
in Lent, when children give cards and gifts to their mothers.*

# April 1st

You could
have fooled me.
The sun
came out
at playtime
then went
in again.

The wind
blew me off my bike.
It made my ears
ache!
It thrashed
the daffodils.
They looked bleak
and perished
their noses
to the ground.
And then it snowed.
Hard.

It's light later
though.
And time for play
after tea.
A blackbird sings.
He's a fool
as well.
He thinks
it's spring.

*Ann Bonner*

*April 1st is All Fools' Day, when people play tricks on each other. In France, a person who is tricked is called a poisson d'Avril – an April fish!*

# *All Fools' Day*

First voice: Look you bicycle wheel
turning round!
When you look down
you feel like a clown.

Chorus: *Yay, Yay,*
*Today is All Fools' Day*!

Second voice: Look you drop a penny
pon the ground!
When you think you lucky
and look down,
Not a thing like money
pon the ground.

Chorus: *Yay, Yay,*
*Today is All Fools' Day*!

Third voice: Look you shoelace loose out!
When you hear the shout
and look down at you shoe
It ain't true, it ain't true.

Chorus: *Yay, Yay,*
*Today is All Fools' Day*!

Fourth voice: Look you mother calling you!
Look you mother calling you!
Is true, is true, is true!

First voice: Well let she call till she blue
I ain't going nowhay.
You ain't ketching me this time
Today is All Fools' Day.

Mother's voice: Kenrick! Kenrick! Kenrrriicckk!
See how long I calling this boy
and he playing he ain't hear.
When he come I gon cut he tail!

*John Agard*

## School dinner menu for 1st of April

| | |
|---|---|
| Solid | soup |
| Grilled | carrots |
| Roast | cabbage |
| Molten | beans |
| Drowned | potatoes |
| Fried | gravy |
| Scorched | bread |
| Baked | butter |
| Hot | ice-cream |
| Sodden | biscuits |
| Stewed | cheese |
| Toasted | tea |

Eat the lot
That's the rule

Knock it back

APRIL FOOL!

Wes Magee

## Seder

Why celebrate with bitter herbs,
salt tears of still-remembered slaves
and (though there's time now
for less hasty ways)
this joyless bread?

*The salt reminds us still
of parting seas,
and, though there's time now,
once was none;
whilst plague took
Egypt's eldest sons
we brought to safety
our firstborn.*

*Pass over, Death;
Pass over, Death;
Passover . . . . .*

*Judith Nicholls*

*The seder is a special dinner eaten by Jewish families at Passover. It commemorates
how 3,300 years ago the Jews fled from slavery in Egypt, when the waters of the Red
Sea parted to let them across. They eat matzah, a flat unleavened bread to recall how
hastily the Jews left Egypt, not waiting for their bread to rise.*

# Palm Sunday

That one day in Jerusalem
a man went riding in
along a welcome path of palms
to celebrate the Passover.

This Saturday in Redditch Centre
shoppers shuttle by
beneath redundant palm leaves
safely out of reach.

That one day hoof and sandal
turned the palm leaves underfoot
to print a welcome message
across two thousand years.

This Saturday no eyes look back
or lift beyond shopwindow height;
and decorative palms
will neither praise them nor condemn.

Today into imagination come
those folded palm leaf crosses
given out in Sunday School.
I pinned them pointing down

the ages back to Calvary.
We should maybe blade them
pointing upward, poised
to scratch a meaning back to life.

*Barrie Wade*

*On Palm Sunday, Christians remember Jesus's entry into Jerusalem when people waved palm branches in greeting and laid them along his path. Palm-leaf crosses are often handed out and palms blessed during church services.*

## The Birthday of Buddha

With my elder brother and younger sister
I, the youngest son, Chiaki, aged eleven,
accompany father, mother, elder sister
to the small temple at the end of our street.

At the other end of our street hangs like an old
wood-block print, beyond the grey tiled roofs
of little shops and houses, our divine Mount Fuji –
a lucky omen for this holy day – for Fuji-san
too often hides himself in smog or clouds.
But today the lingering last snows on his sacred peak
are sparkling in the pure blue heavens.

We are all wearing our best clothes –
my mother and sisters in bright spring kimono and zori,
we three men in good suits, shirts, ties, shoes.
But my father's carrying a folding paper fan.

At the temple gate, the smiling priest
bows his welcome, and we all bow deeply in return.
He sometimes plays baseball with us, but today
he is wearing formal robes.

We bow to the statue of the infant Buddha
standing inside his miniature temple
of spring greenery and pale-rose cherry-blossom.
He is shining in the happy sun. One by one,
we slowly pour over him ladles of sweet brown tea.
He always seems to enjoy it. He, too, is smiling.

The priest and his wife and children invite us
to take tea, the same festive tea we gave the Buddha,
with sweet cakes, satsumas and candies.

With folded hands, we bow farewell to Buddha,
and to the smiling priest, who bows farewell to us.

– But once outside the temple gate
my older brother and I dash home to change our clothes
for baseball practice in the field behind the temple,
where the infant Buddha goes on smiling
as if he, too, is on our team.

And at the end of our street, old Fuji-san
hangs like a crimson half-moon in the afterglow.

*James Kirkup*

*Japanese Buddhists traditionally celebrate three anniversaries: Buddha's Birthday,
on April 8th; Enlightenment, on December 8th, and his death, February 15th.*

# *Ching Ming*

Oh, they are cold,
our ancestors
freezing in winter graves,
their bones pecked clean
by a crow wind;
we will share their cold.

Put out the fires.
Dampen the stoves.
Let us feel frost
creep through bone and belly,
binding us to our ancestors
before we bring them heat.

Now light the grave fires.
Bring padded clothes,
grain, gifts, furniture;
sizzle the flames with wine
until warm spirits rise
to wake them from winter.

Our feet will soon begin
the summer journeys,
planting, harvesting.
Here are flowers and fire
for our ancestors;
from beneath the earth
may they be with us.

*Irene Rawnsley*

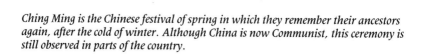

*Ching Ming is the Chinese festival of spring in which they remember their ancestors
again, after the cold of winter. Although China is now Communist, this ceremony is
still observed in parts of the country.*

## Easter

This is the end of Winter's reign
When the squirrel had to hide,
When the swallows fled to the south
And all the Summer flowers died;

When the snow took over the mountain tops,
When the frost had the fields in an iron hold,
When ice shut the swans out of ponds
And the world was imprisoned by cold.

Winter has passed: the birds return,
The seed beneath the stone has found
A way to the light and like a knife
The daffodil prises open the ground;

Buds and bulbs break out of their bonds
And squirrels were only sleeping and survive
By the yearly miracle
That keeps the world alive.

*Stanley Cook*

*Easter Sunday is the most important day in the Christian calendar,
celebrating the day when Jesus rose from the dead.*

# The Dragon's Lament
## (On the eve of St George's Day)

It isn't much fun to find out you're a dragon,
I wish I'd been born St George.
I would laze about town, drinking wine from a flagon,
Then look for poor creatures to scourge.

I'd have a head start with my sword and my armour,
No dragon would *dare* to advance;
And dozens of maidens I'd save before supper,
If only they'd give me the chance.

I'm the last of my kind;
You would think they'd preserve me,
For I'm tired and I'm flameless and old.
I'll give just a few puffs
And then roll over gently
And hope that the blade isn't cold.

St George, he'll be famous –
But what of the dragon?
Who will remember *my* name?
Ah, such is this world –
They must all have their heroes,
And dragons are always 'fair game'.

*Trevor Harvey*

*April 23rd is St George's Day in England. Legend says that St George, the patron saint of England, slew a dragon who was ravaging the countryside.*

# *May Day*

OAK AND IVY, SYCAMORE ASH, WHAT SHALL WE LEAVE BY THE COTTAGE DOOR?
DROP YOUR BRANCH AND SAY NO MORE!
HAWTHORN, IVY, SYCAMORE OAK,
FEAR FOR THE FAIR, NUT FOR A SLUT,
ALDER FOR A SCOWLER, HAWTHORN FOR A FRIEND;
WASH YOUR FACE IN THE MAY DEW,
BRAMBLE FOR THE RAMBLER, PLUM FOR THE GLUM —
WISH, THEN TAKE YOUR CHANCE,
JACK-IN-THE-GREEN OR MAYPOLE QUEEN,
DROP YOUR BRANCH AND RUN, RUN, RUN!
WHO'LL JOIN THE MAYPOLE DANCE?
WHAT SHALL WE LEAVE BY THE COTTAGE DOOR?
HAWTHORN, SYCAMORE, IVY, OAK,
DROP YOUR BRANCH AND SAY NO MORE!
OAK AND IVY, SYCAMORE, ASH.
MAYDAYMAYDAYMAYDAY

*Judith Nicholls*

*May Day – May 1st – is a holiday in many countries. In Britain, some of the old rituals are still carried on, with Morris-dancers and dancing round a maypole.*

## *May Day*

Twirl your ribbons
    as you go
in and out
    the Maypole. . . .
Let the colours
    twist and flow
in and out
    the Maypole!

Skip and rally,
    turn about,
round and round
    the Maypole. . . .
Outside in
    and inside out –
round and round
    the Maypole!

Now, the season's
    crowned and blessed –
all her rites
    attended –
Stands the Maypole
    fully dressed,
and the dance
    is ended!

        And the dance
            is
              ended. . . . .

*Jean Kenward*

## On Mother's Day

On Mother's Day we got up first,
so full of plans we almost burst.

We started breakfast right away
as our surprise for Mother's Day.

We picked some flowers, then hurried back
to make the coffee – rather black.

We wrapped our gifts and wrote a card
and boiled the eggs – a little hard.

And then we sang a serenade,
which burned the toast, I am afraid.

But Mother said, amidst our cheers,
'Oh, what a big surprise, my dears.
I've not had such a treat in years.'
And she was smiling to her ears!

*Aileen Fisher*

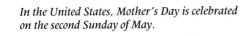

*In the United States, Mother's Day is celebrated
on the second Sunday of May.*

## Cheung Chau Festival
*(Hong Kong)*

Everyone likes
            eating buns
                        but these buns
                                    are special ones.
If you bite one
            I can swear
                        luck will touch you,
                                    anywhere!

Eat a bun!
    Eat a bun!
Come, now, take
    another one!
Buy a bagful
    and be sure
luck will knock
    upon your door!
One
    two
        three
            four –
                I can't manage
                        any more!

*Jean Kenward*

*The Bun Festival on the Hong Kong island of Cheung Chau is held in honour of
Pak Tai, a legendary ruler who is said to have defeated the demon king.*

# Ramadan

The moon that once was full, ripe and golden,
Wasted away, thin as the rind of a melon,
Like those poor whom sudden ill fortune
Has wasted away like a waning moon.

Like the generous who leave behind
All that was selfish and unkind,
The moon comes out of the tent of the night
And finds its way with a lamp of light.

The lamp of the moon is relit
And the hungry and thirsty
In the desert or the city
Make a feast to welcome it.

*Stanley Cook*

*Throughout Ramadan, the ninth month of the Islamic lunar calendar, Muslims fast during the hours of daylight. Special observers, posted in high places, give news of the first sight of the new moon which signals the end of Ramadan and the start of the Idh al-Fitr holiday.*

*Stanley Cook*

# Idh al-Fitr

In the ninth month of Ramadan, one moon to another,
From sunrise to sunset the true Muslim brother,
For love of his God with a faith everlasting
Is steadfast in prayer and is strict in his fasting.

But come the new moon, Ramadan is then over.
It's Idh al-Fitr and each child is in clover.
The boys all so handsome in thobes of white cotton.
The long hours of school for a while are forgotten.

The girls are so pretty in new party dresses
With bright satin ribbons adorning dark tresses.
The mail-box is bursting with 'Happy Idh' greetings
And daytime is taken with visits and meetings.

The sun sinks to Westward, the Red Sea gets redder
As, dressed like a child-bride, the streets of old Jeddah
Are in festival mood, coloured lights brightly burning
Over beach carousel and the ferris wheel turning.

There's presents for everyone, treats and surprises.
There's gold for the ladies and sweetmeats and spices.
Yet one day it's over. Each heart's a shade sadder.
But wait! – Only two months and it's then Idh al-Adha.

*Philip Gross*

*The two main Islamic festivals are Idh al-Fitr, which marks the breaking of
the fast at the end of Ramadan, and Idh al-Adha, the festival of the sacrifice,
which remembers how Abraham was willing to sacrifice his son Isaac.*

## Idh Mubarak!

Maghrib is the name of the dusk
After the sun goes down
And Safuran is the child in the garden
Watching for the new moon.

It's here! The moon's come! It's Idh!
Idh Mubarak! she calls.

Her shalwar-zameeze is like poppies
Her dupatta scarf drifts like a breeze
Her bangles gleam as she dances
Idh Mubarak! she says.

Her family take gifts to the mosque
Today let no-one be sad
Let no-one be left out of the feasting
Idh Mubarak! instead.

At home there are cards and presents
And smells of spices and sweets
And the women rush to get ready
The great Idh feast.

Dad reminds them that under the stars
Of Africa, Pakistan, India,
Bangladesh
This is the day of happiness.
And under
The stars of England, Safuran says,
Watching her moon. Pràise
Be to Allah, Dad says. Praise Him.
And eat!

Bismillahir Rahmanir Rahim.
Idh Mubarak!
Happy Idh!

*Berlie Doherty*

'Idh Mubarak!' means 'Happy Idh!'
'Bismillahir Rahmanir Rahim' means 'Praise Allah and eat'.

## Oak Apple Day

Charles the Second, so they tell,
Hid in an oak at Boscobel.
Later, the entire nation
Rejoiced to see his Restoration,
And named the 29th of May
(Quite properly) Oak Apple Day!

*Raymond Wilson*

*Charles, son of Charles I, is supposed to have hidden in an oak tree after being defeated by Cromwell's army at the battle of Worcester in 1651. In 1660 he was 'restored' to the British throne as King Charles II.*

# On Midsummer's Eve

The night
is hot
and still not
dark

moths make
circles
intent on
the light.

Tonight
we're told
the shy fairies
show themselves

the elves
will dance
round the magic
ring.

What a wonderful
thing!
Whether you
believe
in them
or not.

*Ann Bonner*

*Midsummer's Eve, June 23rd,*
*is supposed to be the most magical*
*night of the year, when you can*
*see fairies, elves and other spirits.*

# Independence Day

Why lie abed when the sun's rising high?
Don't you know that today's the Fourth of July?
Two hundred years ago this happy morn
Our Freedom and proud Independence were born.

These States were united and a striped flag unfurled,
Now known as 'Old Glory' all over the World.
So put on your costume, join the parade
And march with the bands of a great cavalcade.

Banners, streamers and ribbons abound,
Marching bands, cheerleaders from schools all around,
Policemen, firemen and servicemen too,
Boy scouts and girl scouts and a place just for you.

Come to the carnival, come to the fair,
Come to the rodeo for everyone's there.
There's contests and games of every sort,
Baseball, softball, all kinds of sport.

And when it gets dark and you're ready for bed
And the skies blaze with fireworks overhead,
You'll remember your history and think with a sigh,
'How'd I forget it's the Fourth of July?'

*Philip Gross*

*In the United States, July 4th is Independence Day. The celebrations commemorate the signing of the Declaration of Independence, drawn up by Thomas Jefferson, in 1776.*

# The Fourth of July

On the Fourth of July – yes,
    the Fourth of July –
you may run up the flag
    till it's high
        till it's high,
and throw all that you've got
    to the top
        of the sky. . . .

For it's freedom we wanted
    and freedom we sought,
and it's freedom we cherish
    and freedom we bought:
we'll share it
    and wear it
whoever runs by –
    till they know
        as they go
it's the Fourth of July. . . .
    INDEPENDENCE is surely
the core of our cry,
    and we'll sing it, and ring it,
the Fourth of July !

*Jean Kenward*

## The Visitors

'Twenty-seven lamps is what it takes,' he said,
  setting his little candles on the stairs,
'to light the way and welcome back the dead.'
  I helped him light their little welcome flares

because he's my best mate. His Dad and Mum
were Buddhists and I know his Obon feast
means food set out for visitors to come
seeking *Nirvana* which, he says, is *peace*.

'At Obon we invite them to return
  and visit us.' He paused with eyes alight –
like mine, I guess, on Christmas Eve, when wine
is left for Santa Claus. 'They'll come tonight.'

I know his grandad and his mother drowned,
with nearly everybody from their junk,
under the China Seas when bandits rammed
their overcrowded boat. He would have sunk

but for his Dad and sister who took turns
to hold him up. I reckon one who's
rescued from a hell like that soon learns
what welcome lights we can't afford to lose.

'We'll burn the paper lantern now,' he said.
'Grandad used to make them out of lotus
  leaves, but this will have to do instead.'
  I pray and hope it helps them reach us

in these flats. I watch his eyes go still and wide
with peaceful welcome. In the flickering glare
his face is like a beacon lit to guide
the old man and his daughter up the stair.

*Barrie Wade*

*Buddhists believe that at Obon the spirits of dead relatives visit their families. Lamps are lit to show the spirits the way home.*

# Saint Swithin's Day

The lumbering clouds go rolling
round the anxious sky.
A storm wind stirs the willow's
leaves to weep, and sigh.
A distant rumble, deep, of
thunder sends the shy
wren to shelter.
It is the fifteenth of July.

The cruel rain will beat
the gentle rose.
Her blossoms, weighted
with the wet
will droop, and die.
The fretful woods
will moan. The cattle lie
low. It is
the fifteenth of July.

Look through
the streaming windowpane
at rooftops shining
with the rain.
And why?
It is the fifteenth of July.

*Ann Bonner*

*According to legend, if it rains on St Swithin's Day,
it will continue to rain for the next forty days.*

## *Tree Festival*

On the landscapes of Australia
 the weirdest shapes appear,
 so many freaks of nature
 that only flourish here.
There's one found in the north-west,
 no odder sight you'll see:
 a relic of the Dreamtime
 is the mighty Boab tree.
Out near the Fitroy River
 a grim old tale they tell,
 how one great hollow Boab
 became a prison cell.
But now, when wattle's blooming,
 each year the people throng
 to join the Boab Festival,
 for sport and dance and song,
And some will hold their picnics
 near a tribe's Corroboree –
 it's like a kind of tribute
 to the mighty Boab tree.

*David Bateson*

*The week-long Boab Festival starts near the end of July each year at Derby, Western Australia, and it celebrates the grotesque boabab trees which grow in the area. The girth of the trunk may be greater than the height of these trees, which often have hollows inside them like huge caverns.*

# City to Surf

Ten in the morning,
   a packed city street;
   thousands of people
   with fidgeting feet.
A pistol goes bang;
   competitors start
   the long winding race
   from the city's heart.
Tall ones and short ones,
   women and men,
   young ones like Robin,
   Maria and Glenn.
Athletes and families
   all mix with the crowd;
   a few go in wheelchairs,
   stubborn and proud . . .

Past the green gardens
   and up the steep hill,
   through the bright tunnel,
   the runners all mill.
Stride after stride
   as spectators shout,
   onward and onward
   the field stretches out.
Past parks and houses
   and sparkling blue bays;
   now they must feel
   they've been running for days.
Up near the light-house
   on top of the cliff,
   still they keep moving
   with muscles all stiff . . .

Down past the golf-course
    towards the bright beach
    the white foaming surf
    is now within reach.
Feet may be blistered
    yet still the backs bend;
    here's the pavilion;
    it's almost the end.
Though the champ wins the trophy,
    the feeling is fine,
    just crossing over
    that finishing line!

*David Bateson*

*At one of Australia's most popular events, celebrated in August every year, over
20,000 people join in a race from the centre of Sydney to the famous Bondi Beach.
Many thousands more line the 14–kilometre route to watch the fun.*

# Korean Butterfly Dance
## (Nabich'um)

She dances in a robe of white
with long, wide, trailing sleeves.

Her frail neck and neat head support
a red cowl, a strange embroidered frame.

In her left hand, a bright pink peony.
In her right hand, a pure white peony.

As she dances, she crosses those flowers,
transforms a dead soul into a butterfly.

*James Kirkup*

*The Korean Butterfly Dance was originally a Buddhist celebration. In the East the peony is regarded as the symbol of vitality and rebirth, and here it represents the body while the butterfly represents the soul. This dance is usually performed in August, during the oriental season of the Return of the Dead.*

## *August Outing*

The August Bank Holiday's here again,
With buckets and spades and pouring rain;
Bumper to bumper, we haven't got far
Before Maisie is sick in the back of the car;
The baby starts howling, Jim's pinched the last jelly
And Karen remembers that 'film on the telly'
Which she's wanted to look at 'for *weeks* and *weeks*';
Dad loses his temper. Nobody speaks.

After 'single line traffic' and several 'diversions'
We find ourselves trapped behind coach trip excursions,
Five frozen food lorries and, I swear it's a fact, a-
head of us all is a slow-moving tractor,
'Though there's no farm for *miles*. (Each year it's the same,
The tractor is waiting to play out its game.)

Mum's made us a picnic, with boiled eggs and ham,
Which we eat in the car in the long traffic jam.
There's a lull in the drizzle and what do we see
But a space in a layby to brew up some tea;
Then, just as our dad's got the primus stove going,
The sky turns quite black and I *swear* it starts snowing –
Well, sleeting at least. From the stove there's no glow,
And dad's hopping mad, dripping wet, head to toe.

Back in the car, he sits drying his hair.
'We'll make do *without* tea until we *get* there!'
Mum says, 'Let's go home', but now dad's teeth are
        showing:
'*You* wanted the seaside and *that's* where we're going!'

When we get to the sea, there's a mist swirling round,
The car parks are full with no space to be found.
We stop in the High Street; mum puts up her brolly;
We rush to a kiosk and buy an ice lolly.
The sea-front's deserted; the cafés are full;
The amusement arcade isn't much fun at all.
We return to the car and the 'No Parking' sign
And, left by their warden, our ticketed fine.

The journey back home is as slow as a snail,
Bumper to bumper and blowing a gale.
The tractor returns and it drives dad insane
(And Maisie is sick in the back seat again).
We arrive home at last; but there's one thing that's clear –
We're sure to repeat the *same* nightmare *next* year!

(Well, I mean – Bank Holiday Monday by the sea; it's
*tradition*, isn't it?)

*Trevor Harvey*

In England and Wales, the last Monday in August is a Bank Holiday. Families seize
the chance for a last trip to the seaside before school starts in September.

## Today is Labor Day

Today
The machines are idle,
The gates are shut.
The factory stands
Silent, deserted.
The worker's tools
Lie on the bench untouched.
The computer screens are blank.

Today
The laborers sleep late,
Enjoy a day of leisure
In their own honor.
Today
There is no work.
For today is Labor Day.

*John Foster*

*Labor Day, the first Monday of September,
is a national holiday in the United States.
It began in the 1880s as a day in honour
of industrial workers, and today anyone
who works has a day's holiday.*

## *Doll Funerals*
*(Ningyo Kuyo)*

In Japan, so many memorial ceremonies –
for used needles,
> worn chopsticks,
>> broken pencils,
>>> old writing-brushes –

Autumn in Tokyo, at the temple in the park,
men, women, boys and girls bringing dolls –
old dolls, broken dolls, dolls without hair,
without teeth, without eyes, without life,
dolls tormented, chewed by puppies, dolls
no longer loved, no longer wanted.

The Buddhist priest burns incense over
their dejected bodies, rubs his rosary,
utters solemn prayers for their souls.
We, too, offer incense, offer prayers
for those who were once loved companions.

Stacked in temple courtyard, a great heap
of helpless arms, hands, feet and heads;
the monks set fire to this almost human bonfire,
while the bereaved owners brush away tears,
pray, bowing with folded hands.

– But always, before the fire is lit,
they are given new dolls, that they carry home
reverently, to love until the next year's funerals.

*James Kirkup*

*Dolls in Japan are not just toys for children, but works of art, with a religious significance. They were once collected by noblemen, warriors, and samurai. The annual Doll Funeral celebration is part of the Buddhist year. It is usually held in autumn around the equinox – September 23rd – a national holiday in Japan.*

## Nyepi
### *(The day of Yellow Rice)*

Tomorrow is the Day of Silence,
Day of prayer and thoughtfulness.
Tomorrow is the Day of Stillness
And the Day of Yellow Rice.

Why the flesh of many fowls?
Why the rice cakes and the fruit?
What is the food that you are making?
Do we feast this day tonight?

Food for spirits at the crossroads;
Food for temple feasts, my child;
Food for feasting here tomorrow
On the Day of Yellow Rice.

I see blossoms on the roadside;
Frangipani petals fall.
Why the spirits by the crossroads?
Why the offerings by the wall?

Evil spirits come to eat them,
Venture out and eat their fill.
Tonight we drive them back with noises
Till the fields and paths are still.

Will we walk down from the temple?
Will our voices chase them out?
What sounds will we make to drive them?
Can I sing – or shall I shout?

We will sound upon the kulkuls;
We will beat with sticks and hands;
We will strike the gongs and cymbals;
Strike the woks and tins and pans!

In the morning – all is silence;
Gone the noises of the night.
In the morning all is stillness
On the Day of Yellow Rice.

*Trevor Millum*

*The festival of Nyepi is one of the most important in the
year on Bali. It takes place the day after the new moon in
the ninth month, and is a time of purification to make sure
of good crops. Kulkuls are alarm drums which are
positioned in small towers in every Balinese village.*

## Night of the Full Moon

When daylight fades,
    and orange sun dips behind ocean's rim,
    then round moon, round as a silver plate,
    will glow upon the village.
Tide is brimming now,
    sea-water swirls and sparkles,
    fishing boats all safe on the shore.
Inside the house, leaves are ready,
    green leaves arranged by Ibu, mother,
    filling them with fruits and cakes of rice,
    offerings to carry to the temple.
The procession gathers, everyone is here,
    some in clothes of brilliant colours,
    purple and blue and red and yellow.
Now at the temple the drum-beats call,
    the rhythm of the gamelan stirs,
    mixing magical music.
Children are gasping, laughing, clapping their hands
    as puppets throw shadows on a lamp-lit screen
    and men in masks act their story of warriors
    and girls glide in green sarongs with golden sashes.
Far into the night the fire of festival burns,
    eyes grow weary, sleep calls softly . . .
    but dreamy day tomorrow,
    holidays begin.

*David Bateson*

*These festivities take place on the tropical island of Bali towards the end of
September. They provide excitement for crowds of travellers, as well as for those
taking part in the celebrations, which centre around the Hindu temple.*

# Distributing the Harvest
## (A Teacher's View)

We collapsed the tableau carefully,
passing it piece by piece to a class
of kids, arms held up to make their bids
for brussels, for solid and sensible spuds
to ballast the base of baskets,
while the eggs looked on from safe distance,
the tomatoes split their skins and sticky
apples slipped and rolled across the polished floor
to be challenged and captured and pushed
into bags, now swollen fat with harvest swag,
until all that remained were laidback marrows,
stout heroes of the garden patch.
Then burdens were lifted, shouldered and
shifted, till like some desert caravan of
Oriental kings with gifts, our harvest bearers
struggled out, towards the town, across the bridge.
Later we heard of casualties, someone's
cucumber spun under a car, while others on
the farthest run found no one home and hauled
it back or posted produce through letter flaps,
but then we knew nothing of that;
we heard instead, all afternoon, news of
successful missions and watched returning faces,
bright as harvest moons.

*Brian Moses*

*In the past, people held a big celebration at the end of the harvest, known
as Harvest Home, with singing, dancing and feasting. Today, many
schools and churches hold harvest thanksgiving festivals where people
bring food and have special services. Afterwards the food is either sold and
the money given to charity, or it is distributed to old people, hospitals or
children's homes.*

## Harvest Moon

She comes in silence,
over creaking barley
spreading her smooth and silver
benison.

Apple and damson ripen,
and the bullfinch
gaudily colours all
he feeds upon . . .

Hedges wear painted baubles –
poisonous
or sweet – the moon, uplifted
lightens all:

It is her feast,
detached and beautiful,
the far, cold deity
of festival.

*Jean Kenward*

## The Harvest Queen
### (or Corn Mother, who controls all the seasons)

Since sown
in spring
she's grown.
Sun has warmed
and rains
have fed her.
Winds have blown.

Crows have flown
above the fields now shorn
of ripened corn.
Drowsy poppies shown
their dazzling red.

Blackberries glisten.
Swallows gather
from the eaves.
The sheaves
of wheat collected.
The first leaves fall.

The golden corn
is Queen of all
the Harvest. The store
is full. Winter is
provided for.

*Ann Bonner*

## All Hallows' Eve

Listen! There's a sound
out there in the night.
Not the howl of a
dog or the bark
of a fox; nor the squeak
of a harmless mouse.
Nor the shriek
of an owl
in flight.

Not the mutter
of the wind. Not the
whisper of dry leaves
in the gutter.
Nor the waving of the
trees and creaking
of a branch in the fitful,
pale moonlight.

When midnight strikes
be safe in your beds for
it's then that the witches
will ride. Lock all your
doors. Make fast
the windowlatch. Not
a chink of light
must be seen. Tonight
the ghosts will rise.
For tonight
is Hallowe'en.

*Ann Bonner*

*October 31st, the eve of All Saints' Day, is known as All Hallows' Eve or*
*Hallowe'en, when the spirits of the dead are said to rise. In Britain and North*
*America, children celebrate Hallowe'en by dressing up and calling at people's homes*
*for a 'trick or treat': the occupants should give a 'treat' or else they receive a 'trick'.*

# *Hallowe'en*

Hallowe'en, they say,
Was when the witches
Took off on their broomsticks
And flew them up and away
For a night of wicked tricks,
A night to watch
Their silhouettes pass
Across the moon's pale face
And the frightened stars;

Or at a furious pace
They rode on coal-black cats
Grown into mighty horses
To a midnight meeting place.

Hot eyes of demons
Flickered in the dark
Like the light of the candle
Inside this turnip lantern.

Though it's only a turnip
I hollowed out with a knife
There's something weird
About those yellow eyes:
I wouldn't be surprised
If all the demons aren't dead
And one reached out of the night
And took back his head.

*Stanley Cook*

## Hallowe'en

it's a black plastic bin bag
that flaps around my shoulders
it's a cardboard mask
that covers my face
and I don't believe in witches
or werewolves or zombies
I'm just out here making mischief
with my mates

shrieking round the keyholes
chanting 'trick or treat' –
a quick way to raise some coppers
or some sweets –
or if they're tight and chase us
they know we'll just come back
and chuck pebbles up the windows
or soapy water in their face

but I don't know why we do it
it's just a laugh
and I don't believe in witches
like I said
but then I wonder what my mates see
every time they look at me –
do I look as strange as they do
in the dark?

and out there
beyond the streetlamps
and the houselights
and the tellies
where the dark fields slide down
towards the river
can't you feel something waking
something watching
something waiting
something crawling up the alleys
while we clutch each other's hands
and watch the flickering candles
in the withered pumpkin heads
go out like dying stars
as we stand and shiver?

*Dave Ward*

## *Remember*

as we sit
and watch the embers
we remember
the weeks it took
to build the bommie
scaling walls
and stripping empty houses
then up and down the street
knocking on every door
to ask for wood
or furniture
the old arm chairs with broken backs
or the wardrobe that's collapsed

the weeks it took
collecting all those
pennies for the guy
pushing the busted baby buggy
with the lop-sided stuffed-sock head
and tied-at-the-bottom kecks
up and down the precinct
begging 'penny for the guy
eh mate?
penny for the guy'

as we sit and watch
the embers
we remember
the night we raided
Jacko's bommie
and the night they raided ours –
broken tables
and a smashed up chest of drawers
passed hand to hand
over fences
along the walls

then all today
we stayed off school
dragging the wood out
from its last secret hide-out
and stacking it up
piling it up
till the top of it touched the sky
then it's like
all those weeks were over
in one sudden blinding flash
from the first match
that lit the kindling sticks
and the ripped-up papers round the bottom
lit the first fuse
for the bangers and the rockets
a flash of burgers and baked potatoes
half cooked in the dying embers
that we rake with glowing sticks now
as we chew the smoky toffee
and remember

*Dave Ward*

*In England, November 5th is Bonfire Night, when people set off fireworks and light
a bonfire on which they burn a figure called a guy. Bonfire Night celebrates the
discovery of the Gunpowder Plot, when Guy Fawkes planned to blow up the Houses
of Parliament in 1605. Children carry their guy around the streets begging for a
penny for the guy, before burning him on their bonfire.*

# *Please to Remember*

He comes to see us every year
when he wants a change of clothes.
Mum's cold fingers take the hint
and she begins to sew.

Round the bottoms of Dad's old trousers,
round the sleeves of his tatty shirt.
Straw and rags to push down the jersey –
and a cap from Uncle Bert.

Last week's papers to give him muscle,
a walking stick across his knees;
punchball head, button eyes –
a nicer guy you couldn't see.

First we trundle him round the streets
dressed in a wheelbarrow;
hearing coppers splash in his lap
like there was no tomorrow.

Next, he finds a house on the Rec,
wooden, with a nice position;
sits on the roof and cracks on
he's a fire-eating magician

starts by scoffing his head off
then has a bath in the stuff;
scrubs his legs and arms so hard
they drop off

then he wriggles down on his bottom;
sits in a blazing tyre, somersaults for fun
and before the last rocket's fizzed and burst
– heypresto – he's gone!

But no one worries. Don't we know
next season sure as November smoke
he'll be round again, to nudge us on
and get Mum's cold fingers humming?

*Geoffrey Holloway*

## Five Haiku

Tantrums of flame gush
from throats of gunpowder tubes.
Take notice of me!

Bones of bonfire shift.
Startled sparks light up skull-eyed
faces in bushes.

Wisp of grey veil floats,
like some weary Guy Fawkes' ghost,
out through night's black walls.

Spent sparklers spear out
in webs of wire weaponry
at anxious ankles.

High over midnight
an insistent arc of stars,
still stage-struck, signs off.

*Gina Douthwaite*

# Divali

Winter stalks us
like a leopard in the mountains
scenting prey.

It grows dark,
bare trees stick black bars
across the moon's silver eye.

I will light my lamp for you
Lakshmi,
drive away the darkness.

Welcome you into my home
Lakshmi,
beckon you from every window

With light that blazes
out like flames
across the sombre sky.

Certain houses
crouch in shadow, do not hear
your gentle voice.

Will not feel
your gentle heartbeat
bring prosperity and fortune.

Darkness hunts them
like a leopard in the mountains
stalking prey.

*David Harmer*

*The Hindu festival of Divali honours the return of Rama and Sita to their kingdom after fourteen years in exile. During the festival, Hindus welcome Lakshmi, the goddess of wealth and prosperity, into their homes. They prepare for her visit by making beautiful paintings with coloured powders on the floor and by setting rows of lamps to greet her, for it is said that Lakshmi will not bless any home that is not lit up.*

## Divali

Ravana's gone,
the demon king has done!
Now once again
with feasting and with prayer
we light a thousand guiding lamps
to welcome Rama here
and bring good fortune
for the coming year.

*Judith Nicholls*

## *Dipa (The Lamp)*
### *(A Song for Divali)*

Light the lamp now.
Make bright
the falling night
wrapped in the leaves
of autumn.

Gone is the day.
Kindle the flame
to burn
in the dark.
Let it show
the way.

Lit is the lamp
of the moon.
Brilliant the stars.
Make them shine.
Let them unite.
Let there be light.

*Ann Bonner*

## Prince Rama comes to Longsight

A hundred points of flame,
Fleet and weave upon their wicks,
On a wet Manchester morning;
But the hall curtains are closed
Against the littered streets,
And incense burns
In a blob of plasticene,
On every window ledge.

The children are changed;
An exotic orient breath,
Has lifted their spirits.

No longer poor and grubby kids,
From the wrong side of town:
Sayed, from Class Three,
Is now Prince Rama,
Splendid in his cardboard crown,
With Nilam-Sita
Trembling by his side,
And Hanuman, the monkey-king,
Fit to burst with monkey-pride.

Will they forget their words?
Will the infants wail,
At first sight of the monster
And its glittering teeth?
No matter.
The legend holds us in its spell,
As in a perfumed bubble,
Lit by lapping flames.

The story moves to its close,
And Miss asks little David,
To please stop picking his nose.
She thanks us for our work,
And says that next week,
Class Four will give
A Chinese Assembly.

The candles are snuffed,
Leaving a greasy smell,
To mingle with the boiling cabbage.
Sir nips the incense out.
We are back in rainy Manchester,
But we are not the same.
Though Sayed is himself again,
Puzzling over
'Rainbow maths – Book Three,'
And Nilam-Sita has been sent,
To fetch a teacher's cup of tea;
Something of Prince Rama
Stays with us;
Sita's beauty,
Hanuman's guile;
Some touch of splendour,
From a fabled land.

*John Cunliffe*

## *Remembrance Day*

Poppies? Oh, miss,
can I take round the tray?
It's only history next.
We're into '45 –
I *know* who won the war,
no need to stay.

Old man wears his flower
with pride, his numbers dying now –
but that's no news.

Why buy? –
because I'm asked
because a flower looks good
to match my mate
not to seem too mean –
[what's tenpence anyway
to those of us who grew
with oranges, December lettuce
and square fish?]
Yes, I'll wear it –
for a while.
Until it's lost
or maybe picked apart
during some boring television news
and then, some idle moment,
tossed.

Poppies? Who cares
as long as there's
some corner of a foreign field
to bring me pineapple, papaya
and my two weeks' patch of sun? –

But I'll still have one
if you really want.
It isn't quite my scene but then –
at least the colour's fun.

Old man stumbles
through November mud,
still keeps his silence
at the eleventh hour.

*Judith Nicholls*

*On Remembrance Day, people wear red poppies to remember those who died in World War One (1914–1918) and World War Two (1939–1945). Remembrance Day takes place on Armistice Day, November 11th – the day when the armistice ending World War One was signed. It used to be the custom to observe two minutes' silence at eleven minutes past eleven o'clock on November 11th in memory of all those who lost their lives in the wars. Today, the two minutes' silence is kept during memorial services which are held on the Sunday nearest to November 11th. In some European countries, November 11th is a public holiday.*

# Remembrance Day

To some
The poppy is the Somme
And blood, dead sons,
Remembrance and forgetting.

To me
It is the fragile wavering hope
Of, one day,
All suns never setting.

*John Kitching*

# The Lord Mayor's Parade

Drums beat,
Bugles blow,
Sirens sound,
Balloons
Burst with a bang,
Bells ring,
Pipes play,
People sing.

All the traffic stops
Or has to go a different way
And people line the road
For the Mayor's parade.

Men march,
Girls dance,
All the vans,
Carts and lorries
Are in fancy dress.

I wave to the parade
And from the lorries
That look like castles,
Space ships,
Monsters,
Houses,
Or desert islands,
The Lord Mayor's friends
Wave back to me.

*Stanley Cook*

*Every autumn a new Lord Mayor of London takes office. The Lord Mayor's
Show is a parade of bands and floats through London's streets.*

# We Each Wore Half a Horse

We each wore half a horse,
and pranced in a parade,
and you can guess, of course,
which half of it *I* played.

*Jack Prelutsky*

# *Thanksgiving*

Thank You
　　for all my hands can hold –
　　　apples red,
　　　　and melons gold,
　　　　　yellow corn
　　　　　　both ripe and sweet,
　　　　　　　peas and beans
　　　　　　　　so good to eat!

Thank You
　　for all my eyes can see –
　　　lovely sunlight,
　　　　field and tree,
　　　　　white cloud-boats
　　　　　　in sea-deep sky,
　　　　　　　soaring bird
　　　　　　　　and butterfly.

Thank You
　　for all my ears can hear –
　　　birds' song echoing
　　　　far and near,
　　　　　songs of little
　　　　　　stream, big sea,
　　　　　　　cricket, bullfrog,
　　　　　　　　duck and bee!

*Ivy O. Eastwick*

*Thanksgiving Day in the United States is the fourth Thursday of November. People give thanks for the blessings they have received during the year and celebrate with a special meal. The first Thanksgiving days were harvest festivals, remembering in particular the first successful harvest of the Plymouth colonists in 1621. In Canada, Thanksgiving Day is the second Monday in October.*

# *Thanksgiving Day*

Over the river and through the wood,
  To grandfather's house we go;
      The horse knows the way
      To carry the sleigh
  Through the white and drifted snow.

Over the river and through the wood –
  Oh, how the wind does blow!
      It stings the toes
      And bites the nose,
  As over the ground we go.

Over the river and through the wood,
  To have a first-rate play,
      Hear the bells ring,
      'Ting-a-ling-ding!'
  Hurrah for Thanksgiving Day!

Over the river and through the wood,
  Trot fast, my dapple-gray!
      Spring over the ground,
      Like a hunting-hound!
  For this is Thanksgiving Day.

Over the river and through the wood,
  And straight through the barn-yard gate.
      We seem to go
      Extremely slow –
  It is so hard to wait!

Over the river and through the wood –
  Now grandmother's cap I spy!
      Hurrah for the fun!
      Is the pudding done?
  Hurrah for the pumpkin-pie!

*L. Maria Child*

## *Mela*

Listen to the reading,
    listen to the hymn.
Today it is a holy day.
    Let us think of him
who guided us
    and brought us
from darkness
    into light –
into sudden morning
    out of thick night.

Let us eat together.
    Let us take our ease.
Let us throw our weapons down.

    Here, is peace.

*Jean Kenward*

*In late November or early December, the Sikhs celebrate the birthday of Guru Nanak, the founder of their religion. Two days before his birthday people meet to read from the holy book, the Guru Granth Sahib, and they continue without stopping until the birthday dawns. During the ceremony they share a meal made from flour, butter, sugar and water, and everyone eats from the same bowl as a symbol that all Sikhs are equal before God.*

## December

This is the month
of Advent.
Frosty stars
are magnificent
in the winter
sky.

The robin sings.
Brings
his joy.
Makes glad
the sad
short days.

Ring bells.
Sing the hymn
which tells
of the birth
imminent.

Light the candle.
Count the days.
And wait
for the great
event.

*Ann Bonner*

For Christians, the season of Advent includes the four Sundays before Christmas. Children are sometimes sent Advent Calendars – a picture with numbered windows on it, one to be opened each day in December up to Christmas Day.

## Light the Festive Candles
*(For Hanukkah)*

Light the first of eight tonight –
the farthest candle to the right.

Light the first and second, too,
when tomorrow's day is through.

Then light three, and then light four –
every dusk one candle more

Till all eight burn bright and high,
honouring a day gone by

When the Temple was restored,
rescued from the Syrian lord,

And an eight-day feast proclaimed –
The Festival of Lights – well named

To celebrate the joyous day
when we regained the right to pray
to our one God in our own way.

*Aileen Fisher*

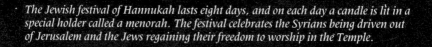

*The Jewish festival of Hannukah lasts eight days, and on each day a candle is lit in a*
*special holder called a menorah. The festival celebrates the Syrians being driven out*
*of Jerusalem and the Jews regaining their freedom to worship in the Temple.*

## Crown of Light Festival

Stars gleaming overhead,
  evening air's clear,
  and Advent is here,
  now in Sweden.
Golden-haired girls
  in each village and town
  wear a white flowing gown,
  now in Sweden.

With a crown of green leaves,
  and candles all bright,
  on St Lucia's night,
  now in Sweden.
Snowflakes are dancing,
  as bells start to ring,
  and the children's choirs sing,
  now in Sweden.

*David Bateson*

*The festival of St Lucia is celebrated all over Sweden on December 13th. A legend
says that Lucy took food to Christians in the caves under Rome, wearing lights on
her head – hence the five candles in the crown of leaves.*

## Winter Forest on Market Street

Here is the tree full of light.
Here is the silver tree.
Here is the tree with the Angel.
Here is the tree full of stars.

Here is the bald tree.
Here is the tree in a bucket.
Here is the tree with its arms tied up.
Here is the tree in the dustbin.

Here is the tree
looking through the window
at the snow.

*Martyn Wiley and Ian McMillan*

On December 25th, Christians celebrate the birth of the baby Jesus in the stable at
Bethlehem. During the Christmas season, families put a fir tree in their home,
decorated with lights, and place presents for each other around the tree.

## A Week to Christmas

Sunday with six whole days to go.
How we'll endure it I don't know!

Monday the goodies are in the making,
Spice smells of pudding and mince pies a-baking.

Tuesday, Dad's home late and quiet as a mouse
He smuggles packages into the house.

Wednesday's the day for decorating the tree,
Will the lights work again? We'll have to see!

Thursday's for last minute shopping and hurry,
We've never seen Mum in quite such a flurry!

Friday is Christmas Eve when we'll lie awake
Trying to sleep before the day break

And that special quiet of Christmas morn
When out there somewhere Christ was born.

*John Cotton*

## Christmas Eve Night

Christmas is when you wake before the light,
Mole up the bedclothes to find what might
Be there in stocking or on bed.
Has Father Christmas been
Or someone in his stead?
Fingers recognize the orange and the nuts,
A book as well is easy to the touch.
But what is this? Its shape will not betray
Its secret, that must wait till day.
So meanwhile, snuggle up,
Pull up the sheets
And wait for the dawn
With its Christmas Day treats.

*John Cotton*

## Questions on Christmas Eve

But *how* can his reindeer fly without wings?
Jets on their hooves? That's plain cheating!
And *how* can he climb down the chimney pot
    When we've got central heating?

You say it's all magic and I shouldn't ask
About Santa on Christmas Eve.
But I'm confused by the stories I've heard;
    I don't know what to believe.

I said that I'd sit up in bed all night long
To see if he really would call.
But I fell fast asleep, woke up after dawn
    As something banged in the hall.

I saw my sock crammed with apples and sweets;
There were parcels piled high near the door.
Jingle bells tinkled far off in the dark;
    One snowflake shone on the floor.

*Wes Magee*

## Scarecrow Christmas

In Winter fields
a Scarecrow sings
the hopeful tune
of lonely Kings.

His empty heart
is thin and cold,
his cruel rags
are worn and old.

But in our home
we sing out clear,
warm words of joy
and know no fear.

In bed at night
we listen for,
padded footsteps
at the door.

In other fields
and different lands,
living scarecrows
reach out hands.

They live beneath
the sun's cruel rays.
They do not know
of Christmas Days.

*Pie Corbett*

## *The Party's Over*

It's late and I'm tired, but I don't want to sleep,
I just want to lie here and think:
Why *did* Auntie Zandra shout 'Scotland the brave!'
When Uncle Brian poured her a drink,
And why did Miss Trumble from down the road wear
That tight bright green dress? She looked just like a pear,
And trust poor old Grandad to lose his false teeth –
The fuss until Christopher found them beneath
Some dinner plates piled in the sink!
I just want to lie here and think.

I thought that the joke in my cracker was good:
When is a door not a door?
I fell off my chair I was laughing so much,
But Nans said 'We've heard that before.'
Oh, Nans: her pink kisses are squelchy and wet,
She smells like old roses, she calls me her 'pet,'
She pinches my cheeks and she smiles when I wriggle,
But when she bent over I had the best giggle –
Who'd ever have thought that her knickers were pink;
I just want to lie here and think.

For lunch I had hiccups, but high tea was good,
Especially when, by mistake,
My second (or third) cousin, Damian Strood,
Sat down on the black forest cake.
I got lots of presents: that robot, two ties,
Six hankies from Auntie and – what a surprise –
Six more from Miss Trumble, from Nans a long vest
Like last year; the presents I gave, though, were best:
Self portraits of me in invisible ink;
I just want to lie here and think.

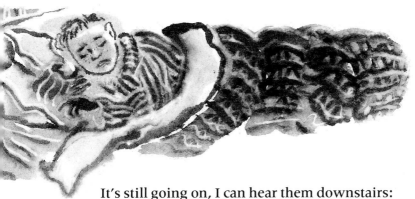

It's still going on, I can hear them downstairs:
A warm rumbly sound like the sea,
I bet Grandad's snoring his head off, so why
Is the first up to bed always me?
Perhaps I'll creep down again, dressed in a sheet,
And frighten Miss Trumble right out of her seat –
She'd wobble like jelly! Or perhaps I'll just go
To stand at the window and wish hard for snow . . .
I'm not really tired . . . much, I won't sleep a . . . a wink . . .
I just . . . want . . . to lie . . . here . . . and. . thi . . . .

*Richard Edwards*

# Thank-you letter

Dear Aunty Grace, ~~Mum said I had to~~
I'm writing this letter just to say
~~I hate that terrible dress you sent~~
I adore the dress you sent today.

~~Erk! Mauve!~~ The colour's just terrific!
Those little puff sleeves are really neat!
Frilly socks to match! It's just too much!
~~I'd rather wear blisters on my feet!~~
Mum says the dress looks sweetly charming.
It suits me now I'm growing up.
~~When I was made to try that thing on~~
~~I really felt like throwing up!~~
The lace around the hem's ~~a nightmare~~
~~I won't wear that ghastly dress!~~ a dream!
I've never seen such pretty ruffles.
~~I hope I wake up before I scream!~~
You shouldn't have spent so much money,
but thanks for such a lovely surprise —
~~of all the dum dum birthday presents,~~
~~yours, Aunty Grace, easily takes first prize!~~
You're very generous. ~~With some luck~~
~~I can lose the socks.~~ So thanks again
~~ink spilled on mauve I hope won't wash out~~
for the wonderful dress! Love from
*Jane*
x x

*Robin Klein*

## My Dad Said

Today is the feast day
of Saint Settee

and on the feast day
of Saint Settee

we must all be quiet
on the settee.

We must not play football
on the settee.

We must not draw with felt-tips
on the settee.

We must not lose our crisps
down the settee.

We must not push the dog
under the settee.

We must not jump screaming
over the settee.

For the wrath of Saint Settee
is a terrible thing

my dad said.

*Martyn Wiley and Ian McMillan*

# New Year

This night
of all the nights
is the year's last.
All, all
the other nights
are gone, are past. . . .

After
the evening, with
its fading light,
put the lid
on the hour
and close it tight.

Close up
your tired eye;
close up the day.
Bid the old year
Goodbye,
and come away.

*Jean Kenward*

# Index

# Index of authors

The publishers would like to thank the following for permission to reproduce photographs:  **Robert Harding Picture Library** *(p 15, 54/55)*; **The Hutchinson Library** *(p 23, 47)*; **Natural Science Photos** *(p 58)*; **Orion Press** *(p 31)*; **Brian and Sally Shuel** *(title page, 78)*.

The illustrations are by:  **Shirley Barker** *(p 8, 40/41, 51, 98/99)*; **Philip Chandler** *(p 43, 48, 106)*; **Katey Farrell** *(p 35, 62/63, 90)*; **Anna King** *(94/5)*; **Alan Marks** *(p 60, 84/85, 102/103, 108)*; **Patricia Moffett** *(p 18/19, 45, 66/67, 82/83, 96/97, 104/105)*; **Jessica Richardson-Jones** *(p 6/7, 17, 26/27, 70/71, 100/101)*; **Rachel Ross** *(p 10/11, 38/39, 74/75, 86/87, 88)*.

The cover illustration is by **Rachel Ross**

# Acknowledgements

The following poems are appearing for the first time in this collection and are all reprinted by permission of the author unless otherwise stated.

**David Bateson:** *Waitangi Day, Night of the Full Moon, Crown of Light Festival.* All Copyright © 1989 by David Bateson. **Ann Bonner:** *February 14th, Shrove Tuesday, April 1st, On Midsummer's Eve, Saint Swithin's Day, The Harvest Queen, All Hallows' Eve, Dipa (The Lamp), December.* All Copyright © 1989 by Ann Bonner. **Dave Calder:** *Jouvert Morning .* Copyright © 1989 by Dave Calder. **Stanley Cook:** *Easter, Ramadan, Ramadan (The moon that once), Mothering Sunday, Hallowe'en, The Lord Mayor's Parade, St David's Day.* All Copyright © 1989 by Stanley Cook. **John Cotton:** *A Week to Christmas, Christmas Eve Night.* Both Copyright © 1989 by John Cotton. **John Cunliffe:** *Prince Rama Comes to Longsight.* Copyright © 1989 by John Cunliffe. **Berlie Doherty:** *Idh Mubarak!* Copyright © 1989 by Berlie Doherty. **Gina Douthwaite:** *Five Haiku.* Copyright © 1989 by Gina Douthwaite. **Richard Edwards:** *The Party's Over.* Copyright © 1989 by Richard Edwards. **Max Fatchen:** *Dragon Dance, Corroboree.* Both Copyright © 1989 by Max Fatchen. Reprinted by permission of John Johnson (Authors' Agent) Ltd. **Robert Fisher:** *My New Year's Resolutions.* Copyright © 1989 by Robert Fisher. **John Foster:** *Today is Labor Day.* Copyright © 1989 by John Foster. **Philip C. Gross:** *In the ninth month of Ramadan, Independence Day.* Both Copyright © 1989 by Philip C. Gross. **David Harmer:** *Divali.* Copyright © 1989 by David Harmer. **Trevor Harvey:** *The Dragon's Lament, August Outing.* Both Copyright © 1989 by Trevor Harvey. **Geoffrey Holloway:** *Please to Remember.* Copyright © 1989 by Geoffrey Holloway. **Jean Kenward:** *Fishing Festival, Mardi-Gras, Mela, May Day, Cheung Chau Festival, Harvest Moon, The Fourth of July, New Year.* All Copyright © 1989 by Jean Kenward. **James Kirkup:** *Carnival in Rio, The Doll Festival, The Birthday of Buddha, Korean Butterfly Dance, Doll Funerals.* All Copyright © 1989 by James Kirkup. **John Kitching:** *Festival, Remembrance Day.* Both Copyright © 1989 by John Kitching. **Wes Magee:** *School dinner menu for 1st of April, Questions on Christmas Eve.* Both Copyright © 1989 by Wes Magee. **Trevor Millum:** *Lion Dance, Nyepi.* Both Copyright © 1989 by Trevor Millum. **Brian Moses:** *Distributing the Harvest.* Copyright © 1989 by Brian Moses. **Judith Nicholls:** *Seder, May Day, Divali, Remembrance Day.* All Copyright © 1989 by Judith Nicholls. **David Watkin Price:** *Saint David's Day.* Copyright © 1989 by David Watkin Price. **Irene Rawnsley:** *Holi, Ching Ming.* Both Copyright © 1989 by Irene Rawnsley. **Barrie Wade:** *Palm Sunday, The Visitors.* Both Copyright © 1989 by Barrie Wade. **Dave Ward:** *Hallowe'en, Remember.* Both Copyright © 1989 by Dave Ward. **Martyn Wiley** and **Ian McMillan:** *Winter Forest on Market Street, My Dad Said.* Both Copyright © 1989 by Martyn Wiley and Ian McMillan. **Raymond Wilson:** *Oak Apple Day.* Copyright © 1989 by Raymond Wilson.

The Editor and Publisher gratefully acknowledge permission to reproduce the following copyright material.

**John Agard:** 'All Fools' Day' from *I Din Do Nuttin*. Reprinted by permission of The Bodley Head on behalf of the author. **David Bateson:** 'City to Surf' from *Orbit Magazine* (NSW Department of Education) 1985; 'Tree Festival' broadcast on *Australia All Over* (ABC Radio) 1988. Reprinted by permission of the author. **Pie Corbett:** 'Scarecrow Christmas'. Copyright © Pie Corbett. Previously published in *Infants Project Christmas* by Scholastic. Reprinted by permission of the author. **Ivy O. Eastwick:** 'Thanksgiving' from *Cherry Stones! Garden Swings!*. Copyright © 1962 by Abingdon Press. Used by permission. **Aileen Fisher:** 'On Mother's Day' and 'Light the Festive Candles' from *Skip Around the Year* (Thomas Y. Crowell). Copyright © 1967 by Aileen Fisher. Reprinted by permission of Harper & Row Publishers Inc. **Amryl Johnson:** 'King of the Band' from *Long Road to Nowhere*. Copyright © Amryl Johnson 1985. Reprinted by permission of the author and Virago Press. **Robin Klein:** 'Thank-you Letter'. Copyright © 1985 by Robin Klein. Reprinted from *Snakes and Ladders* by Robin Klein (1985) by permission of Oxford University Press and Houghton Mifflin Australia. Oodgeroo of the tribe Noonuccal custodian of the land Minjerribah (formerly **Kath Walker**): 'Corroboree' from *My People*. Reprinted by permission of Jacaranda Wiley Limited. **Jack Prelutsky:** 'We Each Wore Half a Horse' from *The New Kid On The Block*. Copyright © 1984 by Jack Prelutsky. Reprinted by permission of William Heinemann Ltd. and Greenwillow Books (a division of William Morrow and Co. Inc.). **Ian Serraillier:** 'First Foot'. Copyright © 1989 by Ian Serraillier. Reprinted by permission of the author. **Anne Wilkinson:** 'Once Upon a Great Holiday' from *Collected Poems of Anne Wilkinson*, edited by A. J. M. Smith. Copyright © 1968 by Anne Wilkinson. Reprinted by permission of Macmillan of Canada, a division of Canada Publishing Corp.